minnie 'n me

GOLD-STAR HOMEWORK

BY Lyn Calder

ILLUSTRATED BY Vaccaro Associates

Disney
PRESS

NEW YORK

Minnie 'n Me: Gold-Star Homework
is published by Disney Press,
a subsidiary of The Walt Disney Company,
500 South Buena Vista Street,
Burbank, California 91521.
The story and art herein are copyright © 1991
The Walt Disney Company.
No part of this book may be printed
or reproduced in any manner whatsoever,
whether mechanical or electronic,
without the written permission of the publisher.
The stories, characters or incidents
in this publication are entirely fictional.

Published by Disney Press
114 Fifth Avenue
New York, New York 10011

ISBN 1-56282-035-4
Printed in the U.S.A.
8 7 6 5 4 3 2 1

This book is dedicated to

Paste your
photo here

Minnie was doing her math homework. She liked math.

There were three problems. So Minnie sharpened three different colored pencils and turned to a clean sheet of paper. Minnie wanted her homework to be just right. She liked to do her work well. And she liked to get a gold star from her teacher.

Minnie read the first problem: "How much is two plus two?"

"That's easy!" she thought. "Two plus two is four."

Minnie wrote her answer in green.

Minnie looked at the next problem It said, "If you have six friends and four ice cream cones, how many friends will not get ice cream?"

"Oh, no! Two of my friends will not get ice cream," said Minnie. She wrote her answer in red. "But we could all share. Right, Fifi?"

"Woof!" said Fifi. Fifi always kept Minnie company while she did her homework. Fifi was one of Minnie's best friends.

"I have one more problem," said Minnie. "Then I can go out and play."

Minnie read the last problem: "If you had three ribbons and your friend asked for one, how many ribbons would you have left?"

"Well, if I *wanted* to give my friend one ribbon, then I would have two left. But if I kept all the ribbons for myself, I would still have three," thought Minnie.

Minnie decided that if the friend were Daisy, she could have one ribbon. That made the answer two ribbons. She wrote it down in blue.

Ding-dong!

Minnie ran to the door. It was Daisy.

"Do you want to come roller skating?" asked Daisy.

"Sure!" said Minnie. "I just finished my homework."

Minnie and Daisy went over to Penny's house. The
three friends skated around the block twice. Then
they went for ice cream.

That night Minnie looked over her math problems. "This is definitely gold-star homework," she thought proudly. She put her homework carefully in her book bag.

Minnie washed up and then took out her favorite
goodnight book.

With Fifi curled up beside her, Minnie read from
her collection of *Wonderful Dog Stories.*

Soon Minnie and Fifi were both fast asleep.

In the morning Minnie dressed for school and had her breakfast. She had a bowl of cereal, toast and jam, and a glass of milk. Then she checked her homework one last time.

"Oh, no!" said Minnie as soon as she picked up the paper. "I got jam on my homework!"

There was no time to copy the problems over, so Minnie wiped the jam off as best she could.

"That's much better," she said. "You can hardly see the jam at all."

Ding-dong!

Daisy and Penny were at the door. The three friends liked to walk to school together.

"I'll be right back," said Minnie. "I just have to get my book bag."

Minnie grabbed her bag and called, "Bye, Fifi!"

On the way to school the girls talked about their homework.

"I didn't like that problem about the ice cream," said Daisy. "It wasn't fair that two of our friends would not get any."

"Don't worry," said Penny. "It was only make-believe."

At school the teacher took attendance. Then the class took turns reading sentences from their new reading books.

When it was time for math, the teacher said, "I would like you to take out your homework assignments now, class."

"Oh, good," thought Minnie. Minnie opened her book bag. But she did not see her homework. "That's strange," she thought. "It was right on top."

She took out one book. There was no homework inside.

She took out another book. No homework.

She turned her book bag upside down and shook everything out. No homework!

"Is anything wrong, Minnie?" asked the teacher.

"I can't find my homework! And I did it. I really did!" said Minnie, tearfully.

"I know you always do your homework," said the teacher. "Why don't you look through your things one more time?"

Minnie carefully looked through everything again. But it was no use.

"Don't worry," said Minnie's teacher. "You can hand in your homework tomorrow. Why don't you help us with the problems at the blackboard now?"

Minnie was glad that her teacher was not angry, but now she could not get a gold star.

At three o'clock Minnie said good-bye quickly to Daisy and Penny and ran home.

She went straight to her room. It looked like it had been snowing paper! There were little pieces of it everywhere. And peeking out from under the bed were two wide, brown eyes.

"Fifi, come out this minute!" said Minnie, angrily.

When Fifi heard Minnie's voice, she did not come out. Instead she hid farther under the bed.

Minnie sat down to think.

"Why would Fifi eat my homework?" she wondered. "She never did that before."

Minnie thought and she thought. Then she remembered.

"I got jam on my homework this morning!" she said. "And I tried to wipe it off, but there must have been a little bit left. Oh, no! What if Fifi ate some of the paper? She could get sick!"

"Please come out, Fifi," Minnie said. "I just want to see if you're all right."

Slowly Fifi slid out from under the bed. Her ears were down. Her tail was tucked between her legs. Minnie was worried.

Minnie looked in Fifi's eyes. They were bright and clear. She felt her nose. It was cool and wet.

Then she scratched Fifi behind her ears. Sure enough, Fifi's tail began to wag.

"Oh, Fifi! I'm so glad you're all right. But you must never ever eat my homework again!" scolded Minnie.

"Woof!" barked Fifi.

Minnie cleaned up all the paper in her room. Then she sat down to do her new homework assignment. The class had to write two pages about a funny thing that had happened to them.

Minnie looked at Fifi. A few little pieces of homework were still stuck on Fifi's coat. Minnie started to laugh.

"Well, Fifi," she said, "you did not help me with my homework yesterday, but you're going to be a big help today."

Minnie wrote at the top of her page, "The Day My Dog Ate My Homework."

The next day Minnie read her story in class.
Everyone thought it was the funniest one of all. The
teacher even gave Minnie a gold star! Minnie
couldn't wait to show it to Fifi.